Welcome to the 2023 Tea & Pearls Sister Gathering:

FLR Global Institute, LLC

Your Intimate Path Retreat

FLR Global institute, LLC
Feminine Life Rebuilders, (501c3)

This Notebook belongs to:

2023 Your Intimate Path Retreat

ISBN:

Sponsored by:

FLR Global Institute, LLC

Proceeds help domestic violence victims, survivors, and those at risk through donations to:
Feminine Life Rebuilders, Inc (501c3)

Your Intimate Path

A message from Andrea, Master DV H.E.L.P. Coach

Your journey of intimate path is a Warriors Journey. I is the walk through the battle of harm to harmony. This weekend together we will explore what you need to win the battle. Be prepared to experience another level of the 3B's: Breakdown, Breakthrough and Buildup.

Whether you are here for your physical, mental or spiritual healing journey and you are ready for the next level, you have made a great decision to be here. Each day has been organized to give you tools for healing. Whether you have experienced the trauma of domestic violence or another traumatic event, the key to living a productive life is increasing your level of resilience and loving yourself.

This is a safe space for you to express your emotions, share your stories and bond with likeminded women. We are all here to create harmony in our lives. The type of harmony that allows us to step out boldly into our mission, walk with confidence, speak with the fruits of the Spirit and perform with dignity.

Show me the right path, O Lord; point out the road for me to follow. Psalms 25 NLT

Eradicating Domestic Violence
by supporting the servant leaders
along their intimate path.

Hold Your Cup, Andrea's Pouring Tea

Day One

Registration

Networking

- *The Battle* .... Andrea
- *Free to Serve* .... Tanyka
- *The Warrior* .... Andrea
- *Lunch*
- *Excelerate - Her* .... Sintrel
- *Break*
- *Restarting Your Story* .... April
- *Untold Story Workshop* .... Jacqueline
- *Dinner*

Day Two

- *Day 2 Introduction* .... Andrea
- *"Rhythmik" Release* .... Nicole
- *Beyond Self-Care* .... Dr. Patricia
- *Lunch*
- *Healing as an Occupation* .... Charley
- *Break*
- *Healing Oils of the Bible* .... Andrea
- *Dinner*

Day Three

- *The Meeting at the Well*
- *The Stronghold of Hope*
- *The Mission*

2023 Your Intimate Path Retreat

FLRGI TEAM

Andrea D. Merriman

Grace Merriman   Katrina Sturdivant

2023 Your Intimate Path Retreat

Sherre Bishop

April Nowlin

2
0
2
3

Charley Cross,
OT

Diane Martin

S
p
e
a
k
e
r
s

Jacqueline
Thompson

Nicole LaShea',
RN

2023 Your Intimate Path Retreat

2
0
2
3

Dr. Patricia
Evans-Morrisey

Sintrel Dass

Tanyka Abbott,
LCSW, CPLC

S
p
e
a
k
e
r
s

About Andrea

Mother, Keynote Speaker, Trainer, Certified Coaching Specialist, Advocate for Life Ownership and Master Domestic Violence H.E.L.P. Coach

Andrea knows to eradicate domestic violence; you need to disrupt the normalcy of violence against women.

Andrea Merriman has survived the death of two daughters working through the pain with passion as she builds a legacy. Working diligently to raise her surviving children she organizes her day as she walks in her purpose, by sharing her techniques and source of strength with women from their youth up.

With over twenty years in Human Resources Management and Customer Focus experience, she has developed two signature programs specifically for women ready to move forward after tough times. She has also been assigned the mission of sharing with the faith-based community tools to becoming a Stronghold of Hope.
Each program offers a holistic approach to healing after tragedy.

Creative Harmony Mastermind™ is a comprehensive program that facilitates self-harmony. It gives steps to get through the tough times and manage day to day task. Techniques learned will range from meditation techniques, essential oil use, time management skills to empower the participant. Learn to walk through your spiritual garden and turn your harm to harmony.

Jennifer Y. Merriman H.E.L.P. Program® offers Hope, Empowerment, Life Skills and Prevention methods to domestic violence survivors and those at risk. Upon completing this unique, innovative program participant will understand the importance of being their independent authentic self, which will enable them to lead a life that is productive and free of abuse.

Because of overwhelming results with the program, Andrea is now offering a Domestic Violence H.E.L.P. Coach Certification. This program allows advocates, ministers and servant leaders to become experts in life ownership so they can in turn teach their clients how to rebuild their lives after abuse and have a sustainable future.

Andrea is an author of 10 publications including: H.E.L.P. Harmony and Happiness Journal, Serving from the Kettle, Serving from the Kettle Planner, The Alabaster Box, The Harmony Series, the Jennifer Y. Merriman H.E.L.P. playbooks and Co-Author of Diary of a People Pleaser.

Andrea is Producer of the Tea & Pearls Sister Gatherings. We invite you to host one of these events in your area. When you do, Andrea will help walk you through the production and how you can bring change in your community.

To work with Andrea, reach out at www.flrglobalinstitute.com or book a discovery session at https://leadercall.motherofharmony.vip/

Sisters I Met Along My Path

Name: _____

Phone: _____

Email: _____

Social Media: _____

I want to connect again because:

_____
_____
_____
_____

Name: _____

Phone: _____

Email: _____

Social Media: _____

I want to connect again because:

_____
_____
_____
_____

Name: _____

Phone: _____

Email: _____

Social Media: _____

I want to connect again because:

_____
_____
_____
_____

Sisters I Met Along My Path

Name: _____

Phone: _____

Email: _____

Social Media: _____

I want to connect again because:

_____
_____
_____
_____

Name: _____

Phone: _____

Email: _____

Social Media: _____

I want to connect again because:

_____
_____
_____
_____

Name: _____

Phone: _____

Email: _____

Social Media: _____

I want to connect again because:

_____
_____
_____
_____

2023 Your Intimate Path Retreat

Sisters I Met Along My Path

Name: _____

Phone: _____

Email: _____

Social Media: _____

I want to connect again because:

_____
_____
_____
_____

Name: _____

Phone: _____

Email: _____

Social Media: _____

I want to connect again because:

_____
_____
_____
_____

Name: _____

Phone: _____

Email: _____

Social Media: _____

I want to connect again because:

_____
_____
_____
_____

Sisters I Met Along My Path

Name: _____

Phone: _____

Email: _____

Social Media: _____

I want to connect again because:

_____

_____

_____

_____

Name: _____

Phone: _____

Email: _____

Social Media: _____

I want to connect again because:

_____

_____

_____

_____

Name: _____

Phone: _____

Email: _____

Social Media: _____

I want to connect again because:

_____

_____

_____

_____

Sisters I Met Along My Path

Name: _____

Phone: _____

Email: _____

Social Media: _____

I want to connect again because:

_____

_____

_____

_____

Name: _____

Phone: _____

Email: _____

Social Media: _____

I want to connect again because:

_____

_____

_____

_____

Name: _____

Phone: _____

Email: _____

Social Media: _____

I want to connect again because:

_____

_____

_____

_____

Sisters I Met Along My Path

Name: _____

Phone: _____

Email: _____

Social Media: _____

I want to connect again because:

_____
_____
_____
_____

Name: _____

Phone: _____

Email: _____

Social Media: _____

I want to connect again because:

_____
_____
_____
_____

Name: _____

Phone: _____

Email: _____

Social Media: _____

I want to connect again because:

_____
_____
_____
_____

Sisters I Met Along My Path

Name: _____

Phone: _____

Email: _____

Social Media: _____

I want to connect again because:

_____

_____

_____

_____

Name: _____

Phone: _____

Email: _____

Social Media: _____

I want to connect again because:

_____

_____

_____

_____

Name: _____

Phone: _____

Email: _____

Social Media: _____

I want to connect again because:

_____

_____

_____

_____

Sisters I Met Along My Path

Name: _____

Phone: _____

Email: _____

Social Media: _____

I want to connect again because:

_____

_____

_____

_____

Name: _____

Phone: _____

Email: _____

Social Media: _____

I want to connect again because:

_____

_____

_____

_____

Name: _____

Phone: _____

Email: _____

Social Media: _____

I want to connect again because:

_____

_____

_____

_____

Highlights from Day 1

_____
_____
_____
_____
_____
_____
_____
_____
_____
_____
_____
_____
_____
_____
_____

Highlights from Day 2

_____
_____
_____
_____
_____
_____
_____
_____
_____
_____
_____
_____
_____
_____

Highlights from Day 3

Highlights from the Weekend

Notes

_____
_____
_____
_____
_____
_____
_____
_____
_____
_____
_____
_____
_____
_____
_____
_____
_____
_____
_____
_____
_____
_____
_____
_____
_____
_____
_____
_____

2023 Your Intimate Path Retreat

_____
_____
_____
_____
_____
_____
_____
_____
_____
_____
_____
_____
_____
_____
_____
_____
_____
_____
_____
_____
_____
_____
_____
_____
_____
_____
_____
_____
_____
_____
_____

2023 Your Intimate Path Retreat

_____

_____

_____

_____

_____

_____

_____

_____

_____

_____

_____

_____

_____

_____

_____

_____

_____

_____

_____

_____

_____

_____

_____

_____

_____

_____

_____

_____

_____

_____

_____

_____

_____

2023 Your Intimate Path Retreat

_____
_____
_____
_____
_____
_____
_____
_____
_____
_____
_____
_____
_____
_____
_____
_____
_____
_____
_____
_____
_____
_____
_____
_____
_____
_____
_____
_____
_____
_____
_____

2023 Your Intimate Path Retreat

_____

_____

_____

_____

_____

_____

_____

_____

_____

_____

_____

_____

_____

_____

_____

_____

_____

_____

_____

_____

_____

_____

_____

_____

_____

_____

_____

_____

_____

2023 Your Intimate Path Retreat

_____
_____
_____
_____
_____
_____
_____
_____
_____
_____
_____
_____
_____
_____
_____
_____
_____
_____
_____
_____
_____
_____
_____
_____
_____
_____
_____
_____
_____
_____
_____

2023 Your Intimate Path Retreat

_____

_____

_____

_____

_____

_____

_____

_____

_____

_____

_____

_____

_____

_____

_____

_____

_____

_____

_____

_____

_____

_____

_____

_____

_____

_____

_____

_____

_____

_____

_____

2023 Your Intimate Path Retreat

_____

_____

_____

_____

_____

_____

_____

_____

_____

_____

_____

_____

_____

_____

_____

_____

_____

_____

_____

_____

_____

_____

_____

_____

_____

_____

_____

_____

_____

_____

2023 Your Intimate Path Retreat

2023 Your Intimate Path Retreat

_____

_____

_____

_____

_____

_____

_____

_____

_____

_____

_____

_____

_____

_____

_____

_____

_____

_____

_____

_____

_____

_____

_____

_____

_____

_____

_____

_____

_____

_____

_____

_____

2023 Your Intimate Path Retreat

_____

_____

_____

_____

_____

_____

_____

_____

_____

_____

_____

_____

_____

_____

_____

_____

_____

_____

_____

_____

_____

_____

_____

_____

_____

_____

_____

2023 Your Intimate Path Retreat

_____
_____
_____
_____
_____
_____
_____
_____
_____
_____
_____
_____
_____
_____
_____
_____
_____
_____
_____
_____
_____
_____
_____
_____
_____
_____
_____
_____
_____
_____
_____

2023 Your Intimate Path Retreat

_____

_____

_____

_____

_____

_____

_____

_____

_____

_____

_____

_____

_____

_____

_____

_____

_____

_____

_____

_____

_____

_____

_____

_____

_____

_____

_____

_____

_____

_____

_____

_____

2023 Your Intimate Path Retreat

_____

_____

_____

_____

_____

_____

_____

_____

_____

_____

_____

_____

_____

_____

_____

_____

_____

_____

_____

_____

_____

_____

_____

_____

_____

_____

_____

_____

_____

_____

2023 Your Intimate Path Retreat

_____
_____
_____
_____
_____
_____
_____
_____
_____
_____
_____
_____
_____
_____
_____
_____
_____
_____
_____
_____
_____
_____
_____
_____
_____
_____
_____
_____
_____
_____
_____
_____

2023 Your Intimate Path Retreat

_____

_____

_____

_____

_____

_____

_____

_____

_____

_____

_____

_____

_____

_____

_____

_____

_____

_____

_____

_____

_____

_____

_____

_____

_____

_____

_____

_____

_____

_____

2023 Your Intimate Path Retreat

_____
_____
_____
_____
_____
_____
_____
_____
_____
_____
_____
_____
_____
_____
_____
_____
_____
_____
_____
_____
_____
_____
_____
_____
_____
_____
_____
_____
_____
_____
_____

2023 Your Intimate Path Retreat

_____

_____

_____

_____

_____

_____

_____

_____

_____

_____

_____

_____

_____

_____

_____

_____

_____

_____

_____

_____

_____

_____

_____

_____

_____

_____

_____

_____

_____

_____

_____

2023 Your Intimate Path Retreat

_____
_____
_____
_____
_____
_____
_____
_____
_____
_____
_____
_____
_____
_____
_____
_____
_____
_____
_____
_____
_____
_____
_____
_____
_____
_____
_____
_____
_____
_____
_____
_____

2023 Your Intimate Path Retreat

_____

_____

_____

_____

_____

_____

_____

_____

_____

_____

_____

_____

_____

_____

_____

_____

_____

_____

_____

_____

_____

_____

_____

_____

_____

_____

_____

_____

_____

_____

2023 Your Intimate Path Retreat

_____
_____
_____
_____
_____
_____
_____
_____
_____
_____
_____
_____
_____
_____
_____
_____
_____
_____
_____
_____
_____
_____
_____
_____
_____
_____
_____
_____
_____
_____

2023 Your Intimate Path Retreat

_____
_____
_____
_____
_____
_____
_____
_____
_____
_____
_____
_____
_____
_____
_____
_____
_____
_____
_____
_____
_____
_____
_____
_____
_____
_____
_____
_____
_____

2023 Your Intimate Path Retreat

_____
_____
_____
_____
_____
_____
_____
_____
_____
_____
_____
_____
_____
_____
_____
_____
_____
_____
_____
_____
_____
_____
_____
_____
_____
_____
_____
_____
_____

2023 Your Intimate Path Retreat

_____
_____
_____
_____
_____
_____
_____
_____
_____
_____
_____
_____
_____
_____
_____
_____
_____
_____
_____
_____
_____
_____
_____
_____

2023 Your Intimate Path Retreat
_____
_____
_____
_____
_____
_____

2023 Your Intimate Path Retreat

_____
_____
_____
_____
_____
_____
_____
_____
_____
_____
_____
_____
_____
_____
_____
_____
_____
_____
_____
_____
_____
_____
_____
_____
_____
_____
_____
_____
_____
_____
_____

2023 Your Intimate Path Retreat

_____

_____

_____

_____

_____

_____

_____

_____

_____

_____

_____

_____

_____

_____

_____

_____

_____

_____

_____

_____

_____

_____

_____

_____

_____

_____

_____

_____

_____

_____

_____

_____

_____

2023 Your Intimate Path Retreat

_____
_____
_____
_____
_____
_____
_____
_____
_____
_____
_____
_____
_____
_____
_____
_____
_____
_____
_____
_____
_____
_____
_____
_____
_____
_____
_____
_____
_____
_____
_____

2023 Your Intimate Path Retreat

2023 Your Intimate Path Retreat

_____

_____

_____

_____

_____

_____

_____

_____

_____

_____

_____

_____

_____

_____

_____

_____

_____

_____

_____

_____

_____

_____

_____

_____

_____

_____

_____

_____

_____

_____

_____

2023 Your Intimate Path Retreat

_____

_____

_____

_____

_____

_____

_____

_____

_____

_____

_____

_____

_____

_____

_____

_____

_____

_____

_____

_____

_____

_____

_____

_____

_____

_____

_____

_____

_____

_____

_____

_____

_____

2023 Your Intimate Path Retreat

2023 Your Intimate Path Retreat

_____

_____

_____

_____

_____

_____

_____

_____

_____

_____

_____

_____

_____

_____

_____

_____

_____

_____

_____

_____

_____

_____

_____

_____

_____

_____

_____

_____

_____

_____

2023 Your Intimate Path Retreat

2023 Your Intimate Path Retreat

_____
_____
_____
_____
_____
_____
_____
_____
_____
_____
_____
_____
_____
_____
_____
_____
_____
_____
_____
_____
_____
_____
_____
_____
_____
_____
_____
_____
_____
_____

2023 Your Intimate Path Retreat

_____
_____
_____
_____
_____
_____
_____
_____
_____
_____
_____
_____
_____
_____
_____
_____
_____
_____
_____
_____
_____
_____
_____
_____
_____
_____
_____
_____
_____
_____
_____
_____

2023 Your Intimate Path Retreat

_____
_____
_____
_____
_____
_____
_____
_____
_____
_____
_____
_____
_____
_____
_____
_____
_____
_____
_____
_____
_____
_____
_____
_____
_____
_____
_____
_____
_____
_____
_____
_____

2023 Your Intimate Path Retreat

_____
_____
_____
_____
_____
_____
_____
_____
_____
_____
_____
_____
_____
_____
_____
_____
_____
_____
_____
_____
_____
_____
_____
_____
_____
_____
_____
_____

2023 Your Intimate Path Retreat

_____

_____

_____

_____

_____

_____

_____

_____

_____

_____

_____

_____

_____

_____

_____

_____

_____

_____

_____

_____

_____

_____

_____

_____

_____

_____

_____

_____

2023 Your Intimate Path Retreat

_____

_____

_____

_____

_____

_____

_____

_____

_____

_____

_____

_____

_____

_____

_____

_____

_____

_____

_____

_____

_____

_____

_____

_____

_____

_____

_____

_____

_____

_____

_____

_____
_____
_____
_____
_____
_____
_____
_____
_____
_____
_____
_____
_____
_____
_____
_____
_____
_____
_____
_____
_____
_____
_____
_____
_____
_____
_____
_____
_____
_____
_____
_____

2023 Your Intimate Path Retreat

_____
_____
_____
_____
_____
_____
_____
_____
_____
_____
_____
_____
_____
_____
_____
_____
_____
_____
_____
_____
_____
_____
_____
_____
_____
_____
_____
_____
_____

2023 Your Intimate Path Retreat

_____
_____
_____
_____
_____
_____
_____
_____
_____
_____
_____
_____
_____
_____
_____
_____
_____
_____
_____
_____
_____
_____
_____
_____
_____
_____
_____
_____
_____

2023 Your Intimate Path Retreat

_____
_____
_____
_____
_____
_____
_____
_____
_____
_____
_____
_____
_____
_____
_____
_____
_____
_____
_____
_____
_____
_____
_____
_____
_____
_____
_____
_____
_____
_____
_____

2023 Your Intimate Path Retreat

_____
_____
_____
_____
_____
_____
_____
_____
_____
_____
_____
_____
_____
_____
_____
_____
_____
_____
_____
_____
_____
_____
_____
_____
_____
_____
_____
_____

2023 Your Intimate Path Retreat

_____

_____

_____

_____

_____

_____

_____

_____

_____

_____

_____

_____

_____

_____

_____

_____

_____

_____

_____

_____

_____

_____

_____

_____

_____

_____

_____

_____

_____

2023 Your Intimate Path Retreat

_____

_____

_____

_____

_____

_____

_____

_____

_____

_____

_____

_____

_____

_____

_____

_____

_____

_____

_____

_____

_____

_____

_____

_____

_____

_____

_____

_____

_____

_____

_____

2023 Your Intimate Path Retreat

_____
_____
_____
_____
_____
_____
_____
_____
_____
_____
_____
_____
_____
_____
_____
_____
_____
_____
_____
_____
_____
_____
_____
_____
_____
_____
_____
_____
_____
_____

2023 Your Intimate Path Retreat

_____
_____
_____
_____
_____
_____
_____
_____
_____
_____
_____
_____
_____
_____
_____
_____
_____
_____
_____
_____
_____
_____
_____
_____
_____
_____
_____
_____
_____

2023 Your Intimate Path Retreat

_____
_____
_____
_____
_____
_____
_____
_____
_____
_____
_____
_____
_____
_____
_____
_____
_____
_____
_____
_____
_____
_____
_____
_____
_____
_____
_____
_____
_____
_____
_____

2023 Your Intimate Path Retreat

2023 Your Intimate Path Retreat

2023 Your Intimate Path Retreat

2023 Your Intimate Path Retreat

*Date:*_____

2023 Your Intimate Path Retreat

*Date:*_____

2023 Your Intimate Path Retreat

Date:_____

Date: _____

*Date:*_____

*Date:*_____

Date: _____

Date: _____

*Date:*_____

Date:_____

*Date:*_____

*Date:*_____

Date:_____

Date: _____

*Date:*_____

*Date:*_____

*Date:*_____

Date:_____

2023 Your Intimate Path Retreat

*Date:*_____

Date: _____

*Date:*_____

2023 Your Intimate Path Retreat

Date: _____

Date:_____

Date: _____

FLR Global Institute, LLC

Vision Statement
To eradicate domestic violence.

Mission Statement
Provide education, services and events to servant leaders that improve social determinants of health, personal well-being and personal growth.

The Company
Name: FLR Global Institute, LLC

History: FLR Global Institute, LLC was founded in 2019 after five years of planning, creating, and building a network of warriors ready to disrupt the normalcy of domestic violence and end this war against our families.

Company Goals and Objectives: Our main goal is to eradicate domestic violence by teaching trauma-based leadership skills in the community and workplace. We strive toward 5/50/5000. Serve 5000 individuals in the next 5 years and have the Jennifer Y. Merriman Program available in all 50 states.

Mission:

Our mission is to provide domestic violence victims and those at risk, training and resources in Life Skills and Preventative measures that will facilitate Empowerment and Hope for a brighter more productive future.

Background:

The Jennifer Y. Merriman H.E.L.P. Program© was developed as a vision to provide a program that fulfills the holistic needs, untouched by any other comprehensive program for domestic violence survivors and those at risk.

Since 2015, this unique, innovative program has assisted women and men in taking ownership of their lives. Each module is facilitated or instructed by a professional with expertise in the topic being presented. Upon completion, participants will have available the tools to embrace reality, make better decisions, and rise above their setbacks. This will enable them to lead a life that is productive and free of abuse.

History of Program Name:

Jennifer Y. Merriman was an intellectually and academically gifted seventeen-year-old. She was on target to graduate with honors with an Associates of Science degree and her High School diploma. Her dream was to further her education and obtain her Doctorate in Psychology. When asked her goal in life she would often say that she wanted to help people in general and teens from dysfunctional families in particular.

On September 6, 2014, her dreams for the future were taken from her when her brother-in-law invaded her safe haven and shot her five times after searching for his wife. This murder was useless and unwarranted. Jennifer had never done anything to instigate conflict or offend the assailant.

With the Jennifer Y. Merriman H.E.L.P. Program©, we are ensuring that Jennifer's legacy lives on. By helping women and men take ownership of their lives, we are helping change the dynamics of a dysfunctional family.

To find out more about how you can bring the Jennifer Y. Merriman H.E.L.P. Program to your area check out or website and book a free strategy session with Andrea or one of our Certified Domestic Violence H.E.L.P. Coaches.

www.jymhelpprogram.com
www.flrglobal.institute/training

To make a donation to

Feminine Life Rebuilders, Inc.

www.feminineliferebuilders.org
or
www.jymhelpprogram.com/donate

To make a referral to the H.E.L.P. Program
www.jymhelpprogram.com/referralform

2023 Your Intimate Path Retreat

Global Mission

Abuse has no boundaries, so we are setting a different standard.

FLR Global Institute, LLC and Feminine Life Rebuilders (501c3) are joining together with other partner agencies and fighting this war on families.

With God's grace, mercy and understanding we will be helping faith-based organizations create a Stronghold of Hope withing their organizations across the globe.

Over the last year we have been sponsoring families and youth programs in Ghana, mentoring women in Liberia and building relationships with organizations in Uganda, as well as conducting workshops, training and speaking opportunities in the USA.

This is just the beginning. With your help we can do so much more.

Meet our Global Team

Cindy Acheampong
Ghana

Cindy is an 18-year old young lady that has a heart for others and love for the Messiah. Cindy ministers to other youth and has groups on WhatsApp.

Richmond Dapaah
Ghana

Richmond was called to preach at the age of 16. He is currently at the University in Ghana where he is the class Chaplain. He also has youth groups on WhatsApp where he holds service and trainings.

Benhynefred Elisha
Uganda

Benhynefred is the Pastor and founder of Higher Dimensions Ministries. He and his wife have a passion for helping youth, particularly young women that have been orphaned or abandoned by families.

Ibrahim Robin F. Kamara
Liberia

Ibrahim is the Pastor of Kingdom Church Liberia. Originally from Sierra Leone, he now resides in Liberia and has a mission to help women become empowered enough to be self-sufficient.

2023 And Beyond

Global Mission

2023 And Beyond

Global Mission

Made in the USA
Columbia, SC
03 August 2023

21134255R00061